PADDLE STEAMERS
A Photographic Legacy

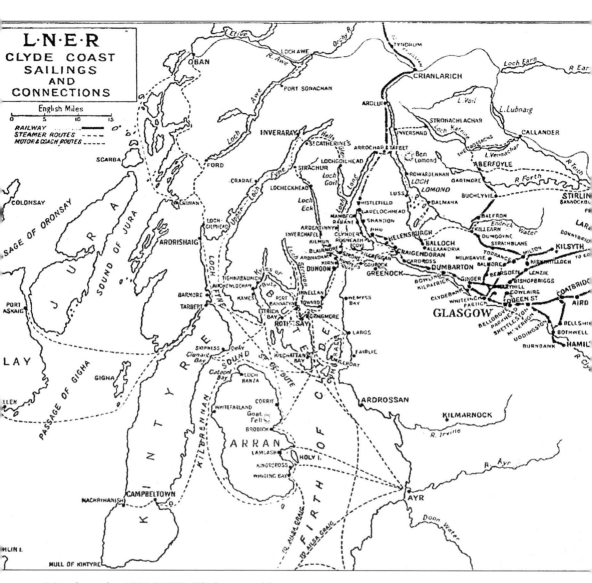

Map from the 1939 LNER Clyde timetable.

PADDLE STEAMERS
A Photographic Legacy

ANDREW GLADWELL

TEMPUS

Crested Eagle photographed from the stern of the *Royal Eagle* at Southend Pier during the summer of 1936.

First published 2002
Copyright © Andrew Gladwell, 2002

Tempus Publishing Limited
The Mill, Brimscombe Port,
Stroud, Gloucestershire, GL5 2QG
www.tempus-publishing.com

ISBN 0 7524 2395 9

TYPESETTING AND ORIGINATION BY
Tempus Publishing Limited
PRINTED IN GREAT BRITAIN BY
Midway Colour Print, Wiltshire

Contents

Acknowledgements   6

Introduction   7

1.   The Thames   9

2.   South Coast   43

3.   Bristol Channel   85

4.   Scotland   99

5.   Elsewhere   119

Acknowledgements

It has been a very great pleasure to compile this book and to work with so many individuals who have given so much of their time to ensure that their special memories are passed on for a new generation to enjoy. I would like to place particular emphasis on the Paddle Steamer Preservation Society Collection as many of the atmospheric photographs in this book originate in this collection. I would particularly like to thank Dr Nick James, Martin Longhurst, John Anderson and the Society for their commitment to ensuring that this special heritage survives. Further information on the PSPS Collection can be found on www.psps.freeserve.co.uk. Many other individuals have given generous assistance and I would like to thank; Peter Box, Pat Murrell, Wirral Archives Service (Cammell Laird Archives), Rochdale Museum Service (Dame Gracie Fields Collection), Southampton City Archives, Southend Standard, L. Hobbs, Charles Turner, Richard Turner, Michael Charman, Maid of the Loch Trust, found on www.maidoftheloch.co.uk, Jean Spells, Waverley Excursions Ltd, Roy Asher, Doug Andrews, Peggy Dowie, Bill Prynne, Southend Pier Museum, found on www.southendpiermuseumfoundation.org.uk, Ian McKinnon, John Beveridge, Olivia Keen, John French, June Bushell, Patrick Taylor, Pat Bushell and not forgetting the mystery man that took the splendid photographs on Thames steamers in the 1930s! I would particularly like to thank Walter Bowie for allowing me to use some splendid images from his collection. And lastly, Richard Clammer for his assistance.

To include every paddle steamer in the UK in this book would be an impossible task. I have therefore tried to portray something of the essence of why excursion paddle steamers became so special and are remembered so fondly. You will therefore find several images of particular paddle steamers and none of others. It is hoped that the variety and quality of images will compensate for the exclusion of a favourite vessel and that the images included in this book will bring back many happy memories.

If you are interested in the preservation, operation and heritage of paddle steamers contact the Paddle Steamer Preservation Society at:
PSPS, PO Box 365, Worcester, WR3 7WH.

Introduction

To many people, there is something very special about an excursion paddle steamer. Even today, it is an impossible task to say what was the greatest of all paddle steamers, as each had its own character and devotees. Perhaps more than any other form of transport these vessels had character to which every passenger felt some degree of love, respect and of course a certain amount of nostalgia. To attempt to cover more than 150 years of paddle steamer operation around the piers and coast of the UK is an impossible task. This book can therefore give just a tantalising glimpse into the magic and atmosphere that our forefathers enjoyed, seen through the lenses of photographers. They are windows into a world that has now disappeared. A world where a day trip to the seaside aboard a paddle steamer was an eagerly awaited treat in a more leisurely age where the fond memories of such trips stayed with the passengers for the rest of their lives.

To find out why paddle steamers became so popular during the latter part of the nineteenth century and the early part of the twentieth century it is important to look at the major social and industrial changes that affected people in the UK during this period. The Industrial Revolution had brought with it a far greater concentration of people living in the great industrial towns and cities. A new need therefore arose for some kind of escape from the day to day drudgery. With the rapid expansion of the railways, the possibility of a day at the coast became a reality and for the first time travel became possible for a large section of the population. This led of course to the rise of the seaside resort, of which many were situated close to the major towns and cities of the Thames, Clyde, Bristol Channel and South Coast. This combined with the emergence of the concept of holiday. Initially workers had the opportunity for short unpaid holidays, but as time passed the Bank Holidays Act, trade union bargaining and holiday funds ensured that holidays became a reality for many.

The seaside holiday or excursion became one of the happiest inventions of the Industrial Revolution in Victorian times, and the seaside pier with the accompanying paddle steamer, became an evocative aspect of it. Many piers had a landing stage and what better way to arrive than by a paddle steamer, upon which you were able to promenade on the decks, enjoy a hearty meal in luxurious surroundings or 'go below and see the engines'? No train offered such pleasures! Paddle steamers were also reflections of the piers themselves. They had a certain style, colour and grandeur and were less boisterous than the noisy steam trains. Paddle steamers became travelling extensions of seaside piers.

Many paddle steamers were operated by local companies that flourished because of their size and knowledge of the local trade. Companies such as the General Steam Navigation Company, P&A Campbell and Cosens all had their roots in nineteenth century England, but survived until the latter part of the twentieth century. Each had its distinct style and knew its clientele well. Passengers would return year after year to travel with the same company and perhaps to the same resort. Victorian paddle steamer travellers were loyal and less demanding than folk 100 years later. Passengers were confronted by a huge array of options. Once a final destination had been decided upon, there were the considerations of which paddle steamer would take you? Would you dine aboard? Who was the captain? What would you do when you arrived at the seaside? These were major decisions indeed when your trip to the coast might be the only day out in the entire year!

Paddle steamers therefore enjoyed an uninterrupted 'Golden Age' where each new steamer became bigger and more luxurious than its predecessor. The novelty of a cruise to the seaside never waned and there was always a yearning to repeat such a treasured experience. The names of *Columba*, *Golden Eagle*, *La Marguerite*, *Lorna Doone* and *Lucy Ashton* are some of the names evocative of such days.

By the First World War changes were on the way. These changes slowly threatened the Victorian paddle steamer. Even by the 1930s, the majority of paddlers were becoming old and more costly to maintain. The rise of the motor car was gathering pace, although it was still the prerogative of the wealthy. The charabanc, although far less comfortable was also offering an alternative. Companies such as the General Steam Navigation Company reacted by introducing a fleet of sleek new motorships. These were indeed luxury ships but could do little to halt the decline that was on the horizon. The Second World War, like the First, brought changes to British society and soon the brightly painted 'butterfly boats' donned their warpaint for an uncertain future.

By the end of the Second World War, many of the old paddle steamers had become war casualties. Names such as *Crested Eagle*, *Gracie Fields*, *Juno*, *Mercury*, *Kylemore* and *Waverley* were amongst those lost. Many wartime losses were quickly replaced with such splendid vessels as the *Cardiff Queen* and the present *Waverley*. Demobbed servicemen were eager to once again enjoy a traditional day trip to the sea. Sadly this enthusiasm was short lived. The motor car, which had threatened the paddle steamer before the Second World War, soon became an option for many people. People's taste in seaside entertainment was also changing and many now preferred the cinema, new holiday camps and walking along the promenade to 'feeding the fishes' on a windy old paddle steamer. Seaside resorts also wallowed in complacency, with many oblivious to the changing tastes of holidaymakers. Despite the Holidays with Pay Act of 1938, people tended to spend this extra time on the new forms of holidays that were emerging. The decline of the paddle steamer quickly gathered momentum. Attempts were made to stop the decline with the formation of the Paddle Steamer Preservation Society in 1959, but with limited success. By the 1960s the trend was unstoppable. Now cheaper air travel introduced cheap package holidays abroad. By 1962, a third of the money we spent on holidays went on those spent abroad. One by one each paddle steamer disappeared; *Bristol Queen*, *Consul*, *Jeanie Deans*, *Medway Queen*, *Monarch*, *Princess Elizabeth* and *Talisman*, the list was endless. Along with these withdrawals went a way of life for so many people. All that people had left now were their photographs and memories. But by the early 1970s, the *Kingswear Castle* had been purchased for £600 by the Society for Preservation, and it was realized that *Waverley* which had spent most of her career working in comparative obscurity on her native Firth of Clyde, was now unique as the last of the line. Luckily for us they both survived and now, in the twenty-first century, allow us to savour what our forefathers enjoyed about excursion paddle steamers. Let us now enter that world and remember some great paddle steamers of a bygone age!

One
The Thames

Golden Eagle was one of the well-loved paddle steamers of the General Steam Navigation Co. fleet (more commonly known as 'Eagle Steamers') that dominated paddle steamer services on the Thames. She had an exemplary war record and during the First World War, steamed a total of 32,140 miles and carried 515,101 troops without incident.

Halcyon passing Woolwich in 1896. *Halcyon* was built for GSNC by J. Scott & Co. of Kinghorn and ran her trials on 9 July 1887. She was built for the Kent Coast service as well as services to the continent and therefore allowed the *Hoboken* to take the daily service to Great Yarmouth. She was sold in 1904 to the South of England Steamboat Co. and finally saw service on the Elbe.

THE ROYAL SOVEREIGN.

The *Royal Sovereign* was built in Glasgow by Fairfields and launched on 17 April 1893. She entered service on the Thames in 1893 and with her extensive promenade deck of 300ft, was a classic and well-loved Thames paddle steamer. Her normal run was from Old Swan Pier to Southend, Margate and Ramsgate. She was laid up during the First World War and then passed to several new owners, before being sold in March 1929, to the GSNC for £5,540 and was placed on the Kent coast service for that year when she made fifty-six trips between London and Margate. She was eventually sold for £3,500 in 1930 to be broken up.

Yarmouth Belle in the Pool of London. The famous Belle Steamers fleet ran services from London to Great Yarmouth as well as Essex and Suffolk and to the Thanet coast resorts. All of the seven vessels in the fleet were built by Denny's of Dumbarton.

A hive of activity as passengers crowd onto the pier at Clacton to join a cruise or to disembark from the paddle steamer and enjoy an afternoon ashore.

Lord Roberts was owned by the Great Yarmouth Steam Tug Co. and in summer months from the 1880s, ran short cruises from Great Yarmouth. She was later chartered to Cosens of Weymouth in 1911 and 1912 before being sold to Scarborough owners and renamed *Bilsdale*.

The *Halcyon* at Yarmouth Quay at the end of the nineteenth century.

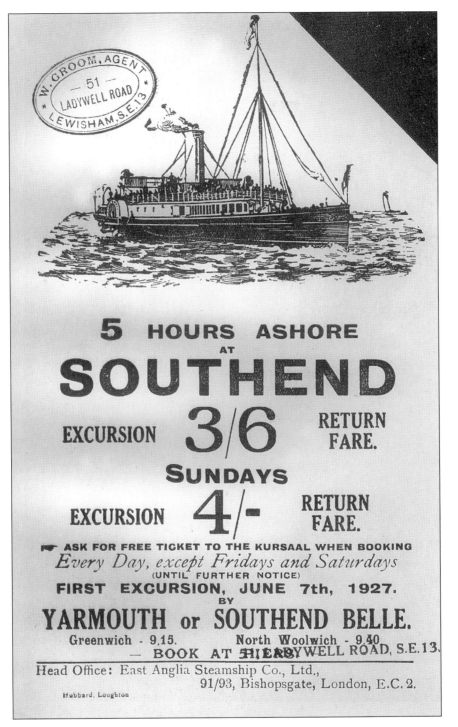

Handbill advertising cruises by either *Yarmouth Belle* or *Southend Belle* to Southend. The return fare allowed five hours ashore and also included a free ticket to the famous Kursaal amusement park which was a favourite attraction for visitors to Southend. Here day trippers would be able to try out the latest rides as well as dancing in the famous ballroom.

Left: Belle Steamers and *Royal Sovereign* guide for 1926. It includes details of all the vessels in the fleet, places of interest along the way and adverts for attractions at the final destination. This particular guide also includes details of the service of the Belle Steamers during the First World War.

Below: Walton Belle was built by Denny's of Dumbarton for Belle Steamers Ltd in 1897 and had a speed of 17 knots. She ran from Great Yarmouth to Walton or Clacton where a connection was made with the London paddle steamer. In 1925, *Walton Belle* was sold and re-named *Essex Queen*. After extensive re-conditioning she resumed cruising to Clacton, Ramsgate and Margate as well as London and the popular dock cruises. She was withdrawn in 1938 and sold in 1946 for further service at Torquay and re-named *Pride of Devon*.

The New Medway Steam Packet Co. purchased the *Queen of the South* (ex *Woolwich Belle*) in 1924. She worked initially on the Southend ferry service before being sold in July 1932 for £300 and soon afterwards was broken up.

The *Isle of Arran* passes under Tower Bridge. She was acquired by GSNC to undertake the popular docks cruises from London in 1933. She was an elderly Clyde steamer that had been made redundant by the building of the turbine steamer *Queen Mary*. She was initially painted with a grey hull and a red funnel with a black top, but by 1934, had been repainted in the GSNC's standard colours. She operated the dock cruises for the PLA on Wednesdays and Saturdays and the rest of the time provided cruises to Margate, Herne Bay and cruises around the Nore Lightship.

Royal Sovereign arriving at Southend Pier. Southend was always a popular calling point for the paddle steamers. By 1925, the astonishing figure of 1,264,000 passengers landed at Southend by paddle steamer. There had been a 60% increase in traffic since 1914. The result was that the 326ft long Prince George Extension was built in 1929 providing unparalleled berthing facilities. The first steamer to use the extension was the *Crested Eagle* followed by the *Medway Queen*. In his speech at the opening, HRH Prince George expected that in the future, the berthing facilities would have to be increased yet again!

Happily the *Royal Sovereign's* paddle box crest has survived and now forms part of the Paddle Steamer Preservation Society Collection.

P.S. " KOH-I-NOOR."   Published by The New Palace Steamers, Ltd., 50, King William Street, E.C.

Koh-i-Nor was built in 1892 at a cost of £50,000. She nearly had a very short career when she ran on the rocks off St David's Head, West Wales, on her delivery voyage from the Clyde. Following repairs, she finally reached London on 2 July 1892. A luxurious paddle steamer in every way, *Koh-i-Nor* was fitted throughout with electric light and had a post office, book and fruit stalls, hairdressers and two bathrooms as well as a promenade deck of almost 300ft. For many years she was the Saturday 'Husband's Boat', making two trips a day from Tilbury to Margate to re-unite husbands who worked in the city with their families, who were able to enjoy rented accommodation at the coast. After the First World War she was sold to Ward's for £6,200 and was broken up at Morecambe in 1919. This postcard was written at Margate on 1 September 1906 at 8.30 p.m.

Laguna Belle passing Gravesend *c*.1935. *Laguna Belle* was originally built as *Southend Belle* in 1896 and later renamed. In June 1930, *Laguna Belle* was placed on a schedule running daily from Tower Pier to Greenwich, North Woolwich and Clacton by her new owners the East Anglian Hotels Ltd. She took an average of 80,000 passengers a year over five years and was usually rostered for eighty-six cruises a year. She carried the distinction of providing the cheapest 'Belle' fares and for being a 'Belle' until her end in 1946. Eagle Steamers purchased *Laguna Belle* in September 1935 and put her on the Clacton and Walton service from Tower Pier until the outbreak of the Second World War. In her days under the GSNC flag, her signature tune *Lily of Laguna* was played as she came through Tower Bridge on her return. In the 1930s there were still many reminders of her 'Belle' days with the old upholstery and the initials C.D.C. (Coast Development Company) patterned into the carpet.

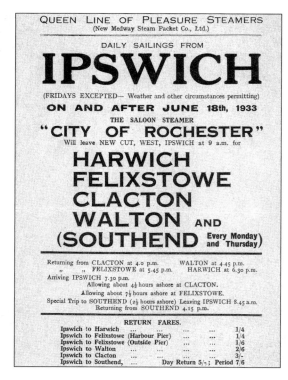

Left: Handbill advertising cruises by the *City of Rochester* in 1933. In 1931, the New Medway Co. had placed this vessel on the service from Ipswich to partly replace the LNER's service, but also to run cruises from Felixstowe to Clacton. Connections were made there with the paddle steamer coming from Chatham and Southend and later that from London and Greenwich.

Top of page 19: The promenade deck being laid on the *Royal Eagle* at the Cammell Laird yard. *Royal Eagle's* engines, which drove the 25 ton paddle wheels effortlessly through the water, were powered by two oil-fired Scotch boilers. She had a total length of 292ft, a beam of 69ft and a draught of only 7ft. *Courtesy of Wirral Archives Service.*

Bottom of page 19: Royal Eagle at Cammell Laird's yard, Birkenhead. *Courtesy of Wirral Archives Service.*

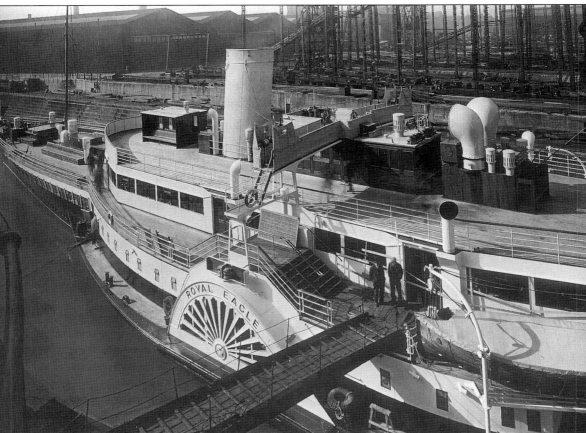

The *Royal Eagle* was launched on a cold February day in 1932 by Lady Ritchie using a bottle of whisky instead of the usual champagne. Guests at the launch included Mr W.J. McAllister, Chairman of the General Steam Navigation Co., and Lord Ritchie, Chairman of the Port of London Authority. *Courtesy of Wirral Archives Service*.

Royal Eagle nearing completion at Birkenhead in 1932. From this photograph you can appreciate the spacious decks and sheer size of the covered passenger accommodation. *Royal Eagle* ran her trials successfully on 30 April 1932, and then made her way to the Thames arriving at Tower Pier on Monday 2 May. For several days she was open to the public for inspection before her inaugural cruise to Margate and Ramsgate on 14 May. On that day, *Royal Eagle* received a tumultuous welcome from all the vessels on the Thames with much blowing of whistles. *Courtesy of Wirral Archives Service.*

Captain Bill Branthwaite was one of the most famous of all Thames captains. He took command of the *Royal Eagle* on delivery from the builders in Birkenhead in 1932, having previously commanded *Golden Eagle* from 1923 until 1931. Although his jovial personality helped to establish the *Royal Eagle*, he hated being late departing from piers and would often show his anger at passengers who delayed his ship! He was very much a personality of the Eagle Steamers who enjoyed having his photograph taken with pretty young ladies (as seen in this picture) as well as running his ship in an exemplary manner.

At the outbreak of the Second World War in September 1939, *Golden Eagle* was one of the eight GSNC vessels to help evacuate children from the danger areas round Gravesend, Tilbury and Dagenham to safer areas at Felixstowe, Lowestoft and Great Yarmouth. *Golden Eagle* was accompanied by *Royal Eagle*, *Crested Ea gle*, *Laguna Belle*, *Royal Sovereign*, *Royal Daffodil*, *Medway Queen* and *Queen of the Channel* in this important work. The journeys on 1, 2 and 3 September 1939 took a total of 19,578 children to safety.

The 1920s saw increasing use made of motor coach transport by passengers eager for a day at the coast. This combined with the Great Depression saw a decline in the number of paddle steamers. By the early 1930s, *Crested Eagle* was very much at the head of the new streamlined services. But the mid 1930s saw the introduction of new modern motor vessels such as *Queen of the Channel*, *Royal Sovereign* and *Royal Daffodil*, but *Crested Eagle* still shone out as the favourite of many passengers.

The visit of Father Neptune to the *Crested Eagle*. The famous ceremony of Father Neptune was often performed on the Eagle Steamers to entertain the passengers and to acknowledge his rule of the seas. Passengers could be 'initiated' on request to amuse their family and friends.

A rare photograph showing the assembled crew of the *Crested Eagle* during the 1930s.

Although the *Crested Eagle* had only been in service for fourteen years, the old small timber deckhouses were removed for the 1939 season and a new modern deck house was erected in their place. It was similar to that of the *Royal Eagle* and may have been a reaction to modernize the ship after the emergence of the sleek new motorships.

The quality and variety of passenger accommodation aboard the *Crested Eagle* was exceptional. The promenade deck ran almost the full length of the vessel with just the Purser's office and the Captain's cabin on the deck. On the main deck was situated a sumptuous dining saloon which included a silver grill serving an a la carte menu. A further two dining saloons and a tearoom catered for a total of 310 at any one time. Light floral designs of upholstery were used throughout rather than the usual gold velvets. Unfortunately, 1939 was the *Crested Eagle's* last season of operation on the Thames.

"EAGLE" STEAMERS

TO-DAY'S SPECIAL LONG SEA TRIP

By the Popular P.S. Golden Eagle

Oil Burning

From Margate Jetty at 2.40

FREE ADMISSION TO JETTY.

SECOND OFFICE ON JETTY

FARE 2/-

Children **1/-**

Under Three Years Free.

THE HAPPY SHIP

TO—

Sandwich Bay

(Near Deal Pier). within sight of French Coast

The trip affords view of Kingsgate Castle, North Foreland, Broadstairs Ramsgate, Pegwell Bay, Sandwich and the Mystery Port of Richboro' and seawards, the Brake and North Goodwin Lightships.

MR. ANSWERS
will be on board to distribute Handsome and Useful Gifts

There is always Carnival on board an EAGLE Steamer
● Book at the Second Office on Jetty for this Trip ●

Tom Whalley
and his Famous Champion Accordionist will also entertain you

Refreshments on board at Popular Prices   Phone: Margate 398.

H. L. TOBY, Printer, Margate.

Entertainment was a popular feature of a cruise on an Eagle Steamer. Here aboard the *Golden Eagle*, 'Mr Answers' was aboard to distribute gifts whilst Tom Whalley entertained on his accordion. Competitions were often held for 'novelty ankles' and for face pulling and there were often competitions to find the stowaways!

Left: The crowded decks of the *Golden Eagle* photographed in the late 1930s.

Below: The magnificent *Golden Eagle* of 1909 was built by John Brown & Co. of Clydebank. She bore many similarities to other paddle steamers that the company built such as the *Jupiter* (1896), *Juno* (1898) and *Devonia* (1905). Like other Eagle steamers, the *Golden Eagle* had her open bridge positioned behind the funnel. Here she approaches a pier with a full complement of passengers *c.*1930. Even by the 1930s when GSNC monopolized the Thames trade, the old traditions carried on. People at Margate often heard a pierman calling out to passengers boarding a GSNC vessel 'No Palace or Belle tickets' despite the fact that both Palace and Belle companies had gone some twenty years earlier!

Overleaf: Passengers aboard the *Royal Eagle* at Tower Pier, London, as the ship prepares for a day trip to one of the Kent coast resorts. *Royal Eagle* had the signature tune of *Open Wide Dem Pearly Gates* that was played to great effect as the large vessel passed through the open Tower Bridge!

The 'Mahogany' private dining saloon aboard the *Royal Eagle*. Private dining saloons for twelve or fifty passengers were positioned on the lower deck. These were a popular feature for special occasions where lobster or fresh salmon were available at a cost of 9s (45p). These private dining saloons were available at a small extra charge and offered 'Liner comfort'.

Royal Eagle's appearance on the Thames in 1932 was perhaps the biggest event of that year for the GSNC. She was well built up to the promenade deck with a 150ft observation lounge and sun deck. She was a popular ship as can be seen here as she departs from London on her regular service to Southend, Margate and Ramsgate. Amazingly, half a million passengers were carried by GSNC on this route during the summer months.

The formidable figure of Captain Bill Branthwaite standing on the bridge wing of the *Royal Eagle* in 1934 as passengers were transferred from his vessel to the *Isle of Arran* because the *Royal Eagle* had broken down. Note the steps covering the paddle wheel and the extended (and open) bridge wings.

When built in 1932, *Royal Eagle* had a black hull, white superstructure and a cream funnel. For King George V's Silver Jubilee in 1935, her hull was painted a lighter colour as seen in this photograph. During that year, she took part in the Fleet Review at Spithead and had her old colour scheme restored for the 1936 season.

Crew members work on the deck of the *Queen of Kent* as passengers look on with interest in the summer of 1928.

Above: An officer towing a log from the stern to ascertain the distance travelled by this Eagle Steamer on 22 June 1935. On that Saturday in 1935, the *Golden Eagle*, *Crested Eagle* and *Royal Eagle* all departed from Southend within forty minutes of each other, offering cruises to Margate, Ramsgate and Clacton with time ashore. Indeed at lunchtime and again in the early evening, Southend Pier was an exciting place to be, as the paddle steamers queued up to embark and disembark their passengers.

Right: Passengers enjoying their cruise aboard an Eagle Steamer on the Thames in the 1930s.

Above: Royal Eagle needed an astounding ten tons of stores each day to feed her passengers and crew. These stores consisted of beer, minerals, ices, meat and vegetables and were delivered at 6.00 a.m. The job of storing the ship took two hours to complete.

Top of page 35: Programme card for Eagle Steamers from the 1930s. Weekly tickets were available for any cruise between Southend and Margate, Ramsgate and Clacton for 15s (75p) during which a lobster tea was always popular.

Bottom of page 35: On the larger Eagle Steamers the crew numbered over 100. The catering department would typically prepare 300 breakfasts and 1,000 lunches and high teas on busy days. Eagle Steamers always managed their own catering, but after the Second World War, the decrease in the number of passengers using the facilities, and rising costs, meant that the company had to heavily subsidize each meal by 5s.

The Main Dining Saloon of the *Royal Eagle*, 1948 season. This luxurious saloon served a wide range of breakfasts, lunches and teas as well as grills and hot and cold buffets. A huge range of drinks was available including champagne, clarets, beers and liqueurs. The catering crew of seventy consisted of stewards, galley boys and stewardesses. During the winter months these people were employed in luxury hotels and aboard ocean liners. Only regular Eagle Steamer employees filled the senior positions such as chief stewards, chefs and second stewards.

Above: Passengers embarking upon the *Royal Eagle* at Tower Pier, London on a busy Saturday for a day out at the Kent or Essex Coast. Tower Pier was opened in May 1929 in the Upper Pool and did away with the need for paddle steamers having to lower their funnels and masts to use Old Swan Pier (which was closed in 1929). A feature common to all Eagle Steamers was the positioning of the navigation bridge behind the funnel to allow the vessels to go stern first up the last stages of the Thames. A bow rudder was fitted for the purpose of allowing the vessels to be positioned ready for the next day's sailing.

Right: Cartoon titled *'Approaching Squall'* one of the forty such images from the book *'Life on the Ocean Wave'* published by the General Steam Navigation Co. in the 1930s.

"APPROACHING SQUALL"

Royal Eagle leaving her moorings before going alongside Tower Pier to embark her passengers.

A sad scene as the *Royal Eagle* lies in pieces as she is scrapped in November 1953. Despite being just eighteen years old when she was withdrawn, *Royal Eagle* was becoming too large and expensive to operate in the rapidly contracting services of post war years. She had been laid up on the Medway since 1950.

Medway Queen departing from Strood Pier towards the end of her career. The closure of Sheerness Pier and Sun Pier along with the huge cost of her survey sounded the death knell for this popular paddle steamer. A company spokesman was quoted at the time as saying that the *Medway Queen* had failed to provide them with any 'jam on their bread' since 1959! She sailed on her last trip from Herne Bay on 8 September 1963 amidst streamers and a civic farewell. There was a public outcry at her withdrawal with much coverage in the press including a series of articles in the *Evening News*. Despite many 'ups and downs', *Medway Queen* has survived thanks to a strong and determined preservation society. She returned to the River Medway in the 1980s in a near derelict state, and now lies at Damhead Creek. Her preservation society have ambitious plans to restore the *Heroine of Dunkirk*.

A deck scene aboard the *Medway Queen* on 31 August 1963. Her master at this time was Captain Leonard Horsham, who commanded her from the completion of her refit after the Second World War until her last day of service when he rang 'finished with engines' for the last time. During the last few days of her operation, he became quite overwhelmed by the amount of publicity that the withdrawal of *Medway Queen* was creating. In those final weeks he gave many interviews on radio, television and newspapers to try and save the ship.

Above: In 1966, the *Queen of the South* (ex *Jeanie Deans*) built in 1931, arrived from the Clyde on the Thames. She certainly looked a fine sight with her red, white and black LNER funnels. Her owners, the Coastal Steam Packet Co. Ltd, had spent a great deal of money and time on preparing her for her new life, but throughout her brief Thames career, she was dogged by boiler and mechanical trouble.

Left: Brochure for the *Queen of the South* during the 1967 season.

Above: In early 1967, *Queen of the South* was dry-docked and further extensive improvements were made to her external and internal appearance including the fitting of a bow rudder. As in 1966, her 1967 season was hit by yet more mechanical problems. She only managed a two and a half week season before boiler trouble halted her on 2 July. On 27 December 1967, *Queen of the South* was towed from Erith to Antwerp for breaking up. *Photograph courtesy of the Southend Standard.*

Right: Waverley positioned adjacent to Tower Pier during a large firework display in October 2001.

In May 1990, *Waverley* undertook a number of cruises to mark the miracle of Dunkirk, fifty years earlier in 1940. She undertook a cruise from Ramsgate to the French coast and on this occasion escorted back the little ships which paraded (perhaps for the last time) into Ramsgate harbour.

Waverley seen from the deck of *Kingswear Castle* during the annual Parade of Steam that takes place on the River Medway in October. As usual on such occasions, *Waverley's* deck is crammed full of passengers eager to greet their counterparts on the other steamer. With a loud exchange of whistles and sirens, the two paddle steamers greet each other.

Two
South Coast

Cosens *Victoria* disembarking her cargo of Edwardian passengers at Church Ope Cove, Portland before the First World War. Cosens' steamers performed similar beach landings at Lulworth Cove and on several open beaches between Portland and Torquay.

Monarch (I) at Alum Bay pier on the Isle of Wight towards the end of the nineteenth century. *Monarch* was ordered by Cosens in 1888 and had an admirable career of sixty-two years before being broken up in 1950. She was a handsome vessel with a raised forecastle deck, which obscured the views of passengers in the well deck who often got an unexpected drenching! *Monarch* can be seen here with black bell shaped tops to her funnels but these were removed by about 1902. The famous Needles can be seen beyond *Monarch*.

Monarch (I) at Swanage at the beginning of the twentieth century. *Monarch (I)* was specially built for cross-Channel work and took five and a half hours for the sailing from Bournemouth to Cherbourg. With the coming of *Majestic* in 1901, she made fewer trips but continued to make frequent visits to Alderney. In those days she could carry 314 passengers on cross-Channel cruises. At Easter 1912, she ran a cruise from Bournemouth to Southampton to view the departure of the *Titanic* on her ill-fated maiden voyage.

Majestic photographed on her delivery trip to Weymouth from the yard of A&J Inglis at Glasgow in May 1901. *Majestic* made her first trip from Weymouth to Bournemouth on 24 May. *Majestic* was built by the company who built the present *Waverley* in 1946 and was the first Inglis paddle steamer with a continuous promenade deck up to the bow. She was commanded by Captain L. St B. Rawle who was the Commodore of the Cosens fleet.

Lord Elgin of 1876 in Swanage Bay *c.*1890.

Photographs showing the construction of paddle steamers in Edwardian England are rare. Here *Princess Mary* nears completion at the yard of Day Summers & Co. of Southampton.

Princess Mary going down the River Itchen prior to entering service in 1911. *Princess Mary* saw service in the First World War but unluckily, after surviving the war, was sunk when passing over a wreck in the Dardenelles.

A wonderful view as *Princess Mary* enters the water for the first time.

Queen entered service on the Cowes run and for excursions mainly from Southampton and Southsea but also to Bournemouth. The upper deck took up the full width of the hull and right to the stern. Her black paddle boxes were later painted white. On 1 September 1908, *Queen* was caught in a bad gale off Selsey Bill on returning from Brighton and was driven onto a sandbank. She was refloated but was then driven onto rocks. She was later salvaged with little damage and no lives were lost.

The *Lorna Doone* arrived for service on the South Coast in March 1898 and spent most of her life in the Isle of Wight area. She was a popular steamer beloved of many passengers but had quite a slow service speed of just 16 knots.

Lorna Doone and *Queen* laid up for the winter at Southampton in the early years of the twentieth century.

Boscombe Pier *c.*1910 with *Lord Elgin* alongside. Boscombe Pier had been opened on 2 August 1888 and was used in a service that linked Bournemouth with Boscombe and Swanage. Steamers to the Isle of Wight also used it.

Solent Queen entered service in 1889. She was a duplicate of *Princess of Wales* and carried out packet services to Cowes and Portsmouth from Southampton as well as excursions round the Isle of Wight and to Bournemouth. *Solent Queen* was scrapped in the autumn of 1948.

Stirling Castle off Southsea beach c.1910. After her purchase from the Galloway Steam Packet Co. of Leith in May 1907, she undertook cruises from Southampton to the Isle of Wight as well as excursions in the Solent.

The Southampton Naval Works built *Prince of Wales* in 1891. During the 1890s, *Prince of Wales* undertook short trips from Southampton to Southsea as well as occasional trips round the Isle of Wight. *Prince of Wales* was finally withdrawn after the end of the 1937 season and was broken up in the following spring.

Cambria leaving Bournemouth. *Cambria* had been sent to Southampton in 1898 by P&A Campbell to compete on South Coast services from Bournemouth and Southampton. She had a fine speed of 20 knots and was the fastest excursion paddle steamer in the UK. In 1902, *Cambria* carried out a mammoth day excursion. Departing from Southampton at 6.00 a.m. she called at Southsea, West Pier Brighton, Eastbourne and Hastings before crossing to Boulogne. She made the same calls on the return and arrived back at Southampton at 1.30 a.m. the next day. The cost of this cruise was just 12s 4d (62p).

Princess Helena leaving Ryde. *Princess Helena* was built in 1883. For the 1909 and 1910 seasons, she was based at Bournemouth. Her funnel was painted red with a black top as well as black paddle boxes and stone coloured deck houses. From 1911-1914 *Princess Helena* operated the Bournemouth to Swanage service. She was finally broken up in July 1952.

Bournemouth Pier was opened on 11 August 1880. In 1894 it was lengthened to 1,000 ft, which enabled it to take two paddle steamers on each side. Here Cosens *Emperor of India* is lying alongside. She had been built in 1906 as the *Princess Royal* and had a long career which ended in 1957. After the Second World War she received a major refit where her hull was almost rebuilt at Portland Dockyard. She was then towed to the upper reaches of Weymouth harbour where Cosens themselves fitted her out, using panelling and furnishings, including teak from the houseboat *Florinda* formerly owned by the famous Edwardian actress, Lily Langtry.

Balmoral leaving Cherbourg for Bournemouth c.1907. *Balmoral* was built at Ayr, entered service in July 1900 and along with *Majestic* and *Cambria*, held cross channel certificates to Cherbourg from the South Coast. Indeed *Balmoral* and *Cambria* regularly raced to the Continent providing an exhilarating trip for their passengers!

Studio portrait showing some crew members of Cosens' *Majestic c.*1910.

COSENS AND Cᵒ S.S. "MAJESTIC" LEAVING CHERBOURG

Majestic had a fine deck, superb saloons and was a good ship in rough seas. Here *Majestic* is seen leaving Cherbourg. On being requisitioned for war service in 1914 she was renamed *Majestic (II)* and sent to the eastern Mediterranean to become a minesweeper. She was sunk on 28 July 1916 near Oran.

Passengers aboard Cosens *Empress* on 28 June 1920. Notice the narrowness of the navigating bridge and the way that it was exposed to the elements.

Monarch (I) and *Victoria* at Swanage Pier *c*.1930.

Taking photographs as a souvenir for passengers was popular with several operators. Here passengers on Cosens *Alexandra* can be seen enjoying a cruise on 5 July 1922. Notice that almost all of them are wearing hats!

Balmoral was built to compete with Campbell's impressive *Cambria*. On entering service on 17 July 1900, *Balmoral* took over the service to Weymouth and Brighton from the *Lorna Doone* and also undertook day trips to Cherbourg. *Balmoral* was capable of 20 knots and a cruise on her could be an exhilarating experience. During her long career, *Balmoral's* appearance never altered, apart from changes in colour. She was scrapped in 1946.

In 1936, the name of the *Queen* was changed to *Mauretania* after a request by the Cunard Co. They wanted to keep the name, held by the holder of the Blue Riband, for a new liner in the future. In 1937, the same paddle steamer had another change of name when she became *Corfe Castle*, as Cunard now wanted their name back for the second *Mauretania*, then building at Cammell Lairds!

Duchess of Devonshire landing passengers over her bow onto the beach at Sidmouth on 25 August 1934. You can see the passengers assembling to walk along the precarious plank to enjoy time ashore. Just two days later, *Duchess of Devonshire* made a more dramatic manoeuvre at Sidmouth!

Like a beached whale, the *Duchess of Devonshire* lies stranded on the beach at Sidmouth whilst youngsters play around her on 27 August 1934. She had nosed onto the beach, having dropped the usual stern anchor while coming in, by which means her bow was kept on the beach. But unfortunately, the anchor dragged and she was washed broadside onto the beach as seen in this photograph.

Cosens' *Victoria* at Lulworth Cove.

Alexandra is undergoing one of her annual refits on Cosens slipway at Weymouth.

Duke of Devonshire at Sidmouth in the mid-1930s. She is about to lower the landing platform from her bow and the gateway has already been opened for passengers to disembark for time ashore on the beach. *Duke of Devonshire* was later renamed *Consul* when she became part of the Cosens fleet.

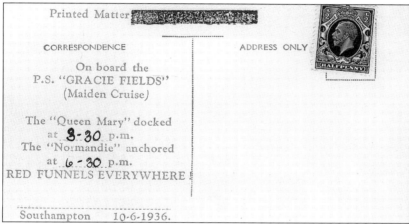

Top: The *Gracie Fields* was launched on 8 April 1936 at Southampton by her namesake, the famous variety and film star of the 1930s. As the *Gracie Fields* glided into the water, Gracie sang her hit song *Sing As We Go* much to the delight of her many fans. Afterwards 200 guests sat down to a lunch at the South Western Hotel where tables were named after principal marks in the waterway served by the operating company. The Red Funnel Co., whose first four ships were called *Sapphire, Emerald, Ruby* and *Pearl* presented Miss Fields with a splendid brooch in the shape of their flag and incorporating these four gems. Unfortunately the brooch was stolen from her some years later. She was also given a silver christening mug and a lifebelt inscribed with the name of her ship from Sir John Thornycroft. The *Gracie Fields* was placed on the Southampton to Isle of Wight service and had just a brief service. She was requisitioned for war service in September 1939 and was sunk on 30 May 1940. Gracie said when her ship sunk 'It makes me feel sad, but as J.B. Priestley wrote, "she went down doing her duty"'.

Bottom: The above postcard was posted on the maiden cruise of the *Gracie Fields* on 10 June 1936. The reverse of the card was printed with details of this event along with the names of the *Queen Mary* and *Normandie* with spaces for the passenger to fill in. The *Queen Mary* herself had only had her inaugural cruise from Southampton just a fortnight earlier on 27 May. There must have been quite an atmosphere as the *Gracie Fields* met the two great rivals for the Blue Riband on that special afternoon in June 1936.

The bridge of the *Princess Elizabeth* in August 1938. *Princess Elizabeth* was built in Southampton and entered service in 1927. She clearly resembled the *Princess Mary* of 1911. She was also one of the last paddle steamers built for service on the South Coast.

Engine Room of the *Princess Elizabeth*.

Sandown was launched on 1 May 1934 and had a service speed of 14 knots. She ran mainly on the Portsmouth to Ryde service and also Southsea to Ryde. She also undertook a number of excursions. *Sandown* was withdrawn and scrapped in 1964 and remained coal-fired throughout her career.

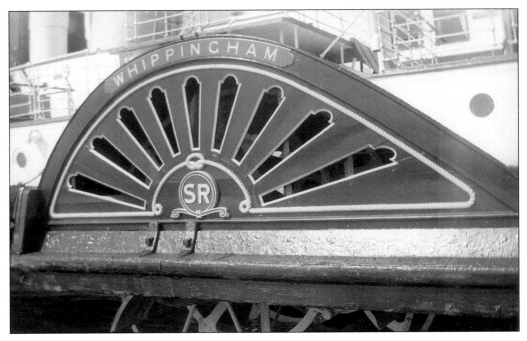

Whippingham's paddle box. The vessel entered service for the Southern Railway in 1930.

Ladies Saloon of the *Whippingham*.

Ryde was the sister ship of the *Sandown*. She spent much of her career on ferry work but also undertook regular excursion work including undertaking some unusual cruises such as the one as the 'floating gin palace' in 1968 in London where the quality of the gin was preferred over that of the *Ryde*! She was finally withdrawn in September 1969.

Ryde's paddle box showing the Southern Railway's initials at the centre of the emblem.

Worthing Belle departing from Littlehampton. *Worthing Belle* was built in 1885 for service on the Clyde as *Diana Vernon*. She was bought by Captain Lee for £3,000, renamed as *Worthing Belle* and commenced service on 4 April 1901 when she offered short sea cruises as well as sailings to Eastbourne and Worthing. *Worthing Belle* continued in service at Brighton until 1913 when she was sold for further service in Turkey.

Paddle steamer approaching the Palace Pier, Brighton. Completed in 1901, the Palace Pier was a popular calling point for paddle steamers. The neighbouring West Pier built extensive new landing stages for the paddle steamers. In the 'bay' created by the new stages, passengers were entertained by spectacular diving acts such as Gladys Powsey who wore a swimming costume with 'Bovril' emblazoned across her chest while imitating a seal swimming. Or they might have stopped to see a display of ants in one of the many kiosks! Not surprisingly, paddle steamer passengers often preferred the varied amusements ashore!

Brochure for Campbell's sailings by *Waverley*, *Glen Rosa* and *Brighton Queen* from Brighton during the 1938 season. On Monday 19 September it was possible to leave the Palace Pier on *Brighton Queen* for a cruise to Ilfracombe, Cardiff and Bristol and to return by train. Cruises were also popular to Boulogne via Eastbourne and Hastings with around five hours ashore in France. Such a cruise would take around fourteen and a half hours with an optional coach tour to Le Touquet.

Glen Gower arriving at Brighton. She made the first post-war sailing from the Palace Pier on 21 May 1947 under the command of Captain Phillips. *Glen Gower* had suffered during the War, resulting in an extensive refit, which included a new bridge and the renewal of most of her promenade deck.

Britannia at Brighton. P&A Campbell started services again at Brighton in 1947 after the end of the Second World War. *Britannia* joined the *Empress Queen* at Brighton in 1948. She sailed mainly to Bognor Regis and Worthing but also cruised to Bournemouth and Ryde. By 1950, P&A Campbell's services were in decline and despite 'no passport' cruises to France being introduced in 1955 (thirty-seven trips that year with 16,000 passengers) the *Britannia* never returned and was broken up at the end of the 1956 season.

A paddle steamer passes Beachy Head and lighthouse near Eastbourne.

Kingswear Castle at the mouth of the River Dart. She was one of four paddle steamers; *Kingswear Castle, Compton Castle, Dartmouth Castle* and *Totnes Castle* that established themselves as part of the River Dart landscape between the First and Second World Wars. Their trips 'Up and Down the Dart' from Dartmouth to Totnes for 1s 9d single and 3s return were an integral part of every holidaymakers itinerary.

The *Totnes Castle* photographed on the River Dart during the 1950s with a train passing on the Kingswear to Paignton line in the distance.

Kingswear Castle at Custom House Quay, Dartmouth on 6 September 1962.

Victoria at Weymouth in October 1952. On 1 June 1946, *Victoria* had been one of the first steamers to resume service at the resort after the War. She was scrapped in the year after this photograph was taken.

Right: The guide to South Coast paddle steamer services provided by Cosens *c.*1960. Details of all the paddle steamers in the fleet along with details of all destinations and local attractions were included in the guide.

Below: Monarch departing from Weymouth. The signs of the steep decline of paddle steamers was evident by 1950 and the first of Cosens steamers to go was the sixty-two year old *Monarch*. This favourite which was well known for her seaworthiness was sold for just £900 for scrapping. She left on her final journey to the scrapyard on 22 February 1950. A new *Monarch* (ex *Shanklin*) entered service in July 1951 to fill a shortfall in Cosens fleet!

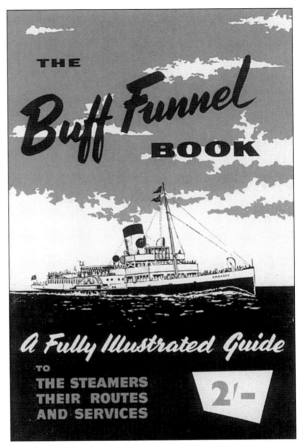

Left: Engine Room of the *Monarch* c.1960.

Below: Monarch's paddle box c.1960 showing the Cosens houseflag at the centre of the emblem.

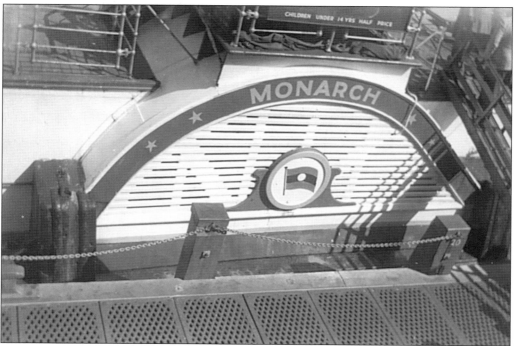

Embassy had been purchased by Cosens in May 1937. She was then overhauled in June and finally entered service in July. Originally, Cosens wanted to name her *Ambassador* but this wasn't possible. In the early 1960s, *Embassy* was able to carry up to 727 passengers with a crew of twenty. Usually running between Bournemouth, Swanage and the Isle of Wight, she sometimes attended Cowes Week.

Above: Lounge of the *Embassy* c.1960.

Left: Engine Room control platform of *Embassy*, 1961. The compound diagonal engines were built by D&W Henderson of Glasgow in 1911 and had a nominal horsepower of 162.

Embassy towards the end of her career in the early 1960s. *Embassy* sailed from Weymouth until 1950 when she was transferred for service at Bournemouth. She was withdrawn from service in 1966. Captain John Iliffe became *Embassy's* and Cosens' last master.

Paddle Steamer "Embassy"

COSENS & CO., LTD.,   **Tel: Bournemouth 24021**

MIDNIGHT CRUISE Every Thursday

WEATHER AND OTHER CIRCUMSTANCES PERMITTING

SOMETHING NEW FOR PARTY OUTINGS with the unique opportunity of seeing the Lovely Lights of Swanage and Bournemouth from the Sea.

(DRESS INFORMAL)

SHOWBOAT

Dancing on Deck

Cabaret

Sing Song in the Saloon

(Fun for the Young and Older)

Depart BOURNEMOUTH PIER 8-30 p.m.

Arrive POOLE Midnight

(Transport Back Arranged)

FARE 11/6 (Special Rates for Parties over 12 persons)

Early Booking at Steamer Office or Pay on Board
Buffet and Fully Licenced Bars Open till Midnight

WAVERLEY PRESS (BOURNEMOUTH) LTD., Lincoln Avenue, Bournemouth

Handbill for a showboat cruise on Cosens' *Embassy* during the early 1960s.

Embassy and *Swanage Queen* at Poole in 1961.

Swanage Queen at Yarmouth Pier on the Isle of Wight during 1961. Built in 1927 as *Freshwater* for the ferry service from Lymington, she was withdrawn in 1959 and sold for cruising out of Brighton under the name of *Sussex Queen*. In 1961 she was renamed *Swanage Queen* and operated for one season on routes from Bournemouth to Swanage and the Isle of Wight. Unfortunately she was not a financial success, and went to the breakers yard in May 1962.

77

A deck scene aboard the *Princess Elizabeth* in the early 1960s.

Princess Elizabeth approaching Bournemouth Pier.

After the end of the Second World War several attempts were made to maintain an excursion paddle steamer service from Torquay. In 1960, *Princess Elizabeth* arrived after her purchase by Torbay Steamers Ltd from the Southampton Co. *Princess Elizabeth* looked as smart as ever as she offered a series of day trips going as far as Lyme Regis and Plymouth as well as half-day trips up the Dart Estuary on most afternoons. The Dart trips faced fierce competition from local boat owners who tried everything to take her trade away. The Plymouth cruises were also soon abandoned because of poor patronage. 1961 continued in a similar pattern but opposition became more intense. At Lyme Regis protesting boatmen refused to ferry passengers ashore, and at Torquay the 'war' became unbearable. *Princess Elizabeth* did not return in 1962 but cruised, instead, from Bournemouth.

Consul at Weymouth on 10 June 1964. Originally built as *Duke of Devonshire* in 1896, Cosens purchased the paddler in March 1938 and renamed her *Consul*. This was in line with the company's policy of 'diplomatic' nomenclature when naming their vessels. During her career with Cosens, *Consul* was based mainly at Weymouth and offered both short cruises to Lulworth Cove and Portland Harbour and longer sailings to Swanage, Bournemouth and sometimes the Isle of Wight.

Above: Consul at Lulworth Cove during the 1961 season.

Left: The exposed paddle wheel of *Consul*.

Above: An atmospheric photograph showing *Consul* embarking her passengers after time ashore at Lulworth Cove in 1961. Notice the somewhat shaky boards and the rope above the passengers' heads to steady them.

Right: A view of *Consul's* stern as she lies in dry dock at Southampton in 1964.

Left: Consul embarking passengers at Weymouth on the first day of the 1964 season.

Below: Consul seen from the stern of *Princess Elizabeth* at Weymouth in the summer of 1964. During that year both paddle steamers competed against each other at Weymouth, *Consul* concentrating on the service to Lulworth Cove while *Princess Elizabeth* offered cruises to the Isle of Wight. *Consul* was withdrawn at the end of the season and *Princess Elizabeth* continued until 1965; the last paddle steamer to operate regular cruises from Weymouth.

Originally built as the *Duke of Devonshire*, *Consul* was chartered in 1963 for cruises on the South Coast and Thames at a time when the number of paddle steamers was dwindling. Her master was Captain Harry Defrates. This handbill shows the short programme of cruise offered from the famous Palace Pier at Brighton. *Consul's* Sussex season was surrounded by problem after problem. In September 1963, Don Rose operated *Consul* on the Thames for a week with slightly more success. This venture with New Belle steamers obviously gave him good experience ready for his eventual operation of the *Queen of the South* in 1966-1967.

PALACE PIER, BRIGHTON
CHANNEL SAILINGS
BY
Paddle Steamer **"CONSUL"**

SPECIAL SAILINGS
ON
SUNDAYS TUESDAYS
AND
WEDNESDAYS

Coastal Cruises		Return Fare	
Leave	Back By	Adult	Child
11.30	12.30	5/-	2/6
2.15	3.15	5/-	2/6
Channel Cruise			
3.30	5.30	7/6	2/6
Newhaven Harbour		Single Fare	
5.45		2/6	1/6

Conditions Weather Permitting (Pier Toll NOT Included in Fares)

FULLY LICENSED BAR OPEN ON BOARD

Kingswear Castle seen from the deck of the *Medway Queen* on the River Medina, Isle of Wight. The *Medway Queen* had been acquired to become the Medway Queen Club, whilst *Kingswear Castle* had been purchased by the Paddle Steamer Preservation Society and chartered to the Ridetts on the Isle of Wight. However *Kingswear Castle* deteriorated quickly, fell prey to vandalism and by the end of the 1960s, her future became uncertain before she was towed to the River Medway to undergo a lengthy restoration.

CAMPBELL'S SAILINGS
from WORTHING PIER
By P.S. "CARDIFF QUEEN"
(Weather and circumstances permitting)

MONDAY, JUNE 8th
9.50 a.m. BOGNOR REGIS (8½ hours ashore) or SHANKLIN (4½ hours ashore) or VENTNOR (3½ hours ashore). Leave Ventnor 5 p.m., Shanklin 5.30 p.m., Bognor Regis 7.30 p.m. Back at Worthing about 8.30 p.m. Return Fares: Bognor Regis 5/6; Shanklin or Ventnor 13/6.

WEDNESDAY, JUNE 10th
11.50 a.m. Special Cruise to SPITHEAD to view ships assembled for the CORONATION NAVAL REVIEW. Steamer returns to Brighton (due Brighton about 7 p.m.) and thence by Rail or Southdown Bus to Worthing without extra charge. Fare 20/-.
Note.—The American Liner "UNITED STATES" arrives at Southampton this day.

THURSDAY, JUNE 11th
11.50 a.m. Special Cruise to SPITHEAD to view ships assembled for the CORONATION NAVAL REVIEW. Steamer returns to Brighton (due Brighton about 7 p.m.) and thence by Rail or Southdown Bus to Worthing without extra charge. Fare 20/-.
Note.—The American Liner "UNITED STATES" sails from Southampton this day.

FRIDAY, JUNE 12th
11.50 a.m. Special Cruise to SPITHEAD to view ships assembled for the CORONATION NAVAL REVIEW. Steamer returns to Brighton (due Brighton about 7 p.m.) and thence by Rail or Southdown Bus to Worthing without extra charge. Fare 20/-.

SUNDAY, JUNE 14th
12 noon. Special Cruise to SPITHEAD to view ships assembled for the CORONATION NAVAL REVIEW. Steamer returns to Brighton (due Brighton about 6.30 p.m.) and thence by Rail or Southdown Bus to Worthing without extra charge. Fare 25/-.

WEDNESDAY, JUNE 17th
3.0 p.m. Cheap Afternoon trip to SHANKLIN (1 hour ashore). Leave Shanklin 6 p.m. for Brighton (due Brighton 9 p.m.) and thence by Rail or Southdown Bus to Worthing without extra charge. Return Fare 11/-.

TUESDAY, JUNE 23rd
9.50 a.m. BOGNOR REGIS (8½ hours ashore) or SHANKLIN (4½ hours ashore) or VENTNOR (3½ hours ashore). Leave Ventnor 5 p.m., Shanklin 5.30 p.m., Bognor Regis 7.30 p.m. Back at Worthing about 8.30 p.m. Return Fares: Bognor Regis 5/6; Shanklin or Ventnor 13/6.

P.T.O.

Left: Handbill detailing Campbell's cruises from Worthing Pier by *Cardiff Queen.* The cost of a day return to Brighton was 4s (20p) and to Shanklin or Ventnor 14s (70p).

Below: Waverley passes the Palace Pier at Brighton.

Three
Bristol Channel

Paddle steamer services on the Bristol Channel were dominated by the company of P&A Campbell Ltd.

Edwardian passengers aboard a P&A Campbell paddle steamer on a cruise to Lynmouth on 14 July 1908. Notice that the passengers are wearing their Sunday best and some are seeking cover from the sun underneath their parasols. A young boy is also selling newspapers around the deck.

Above: Landing Edwardian passengers at Clovelly. Clovelly, like Lundy Island and Lynmouth, did not have a pier and local boatmen rowed passengers ashore under an arrangement with the steamship companies.

Right: Devonia was built in 1905 for the Barry Railway and later entered service for P&A Campbell in 1912. Because of the loss of the *Titanic* that year, extra lifeboats were fitted to the *Devonia*. *Devonia* was lost in the Dunkirk evacuation in 1940.

Ravenswood at Barry docks in August 1935 (Flat Holm can be seen on the horizon). *Ravenswood* had made her maiden voyage on 3 July 1891 at Bristol.

Two passengers pose aboard a Bristol Channel paddle steamer in the 1930s alongside members of a traditional steamer band.

Brighton Belle leaving Bristol after a refit to take up the Cardiff to Weston Super Mare service in 1937. She had been given a new elliptical funnel and a light grey hull. Few people liked the new 'light' colour and she was soon nicknamed the 'Grey Ghost'. The new colour scheme was changed in 1938.

Glen Gower entered service in 1922 and spent the years leading up to the Second World War on the South Coast. After the War in 1955, *Glen Gower* replaced the *Cardiff Queen* on the South Coast so that she could restart the popular 'no passport' day trips to Boulogne. During that year, over 16,000 passengers made the trip to France.

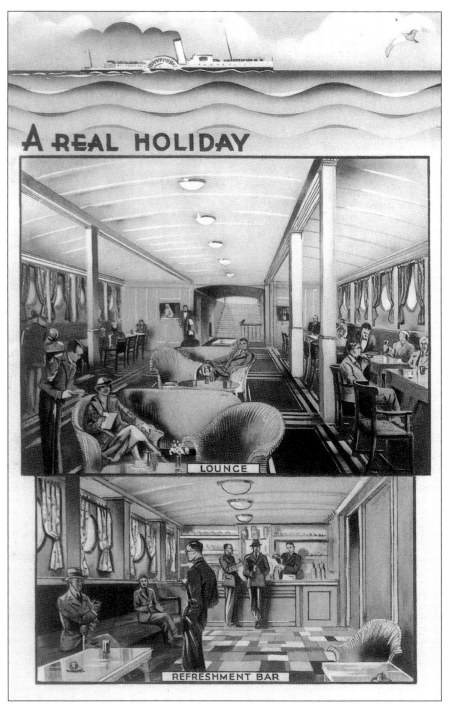

Opposite: Publicity brochure produced by P&A Campbell in the late 1930s.

Above: The interiors of P&A Campbell paddle steamers were luxurious as seen from this 1930s brochure. The menu was likewise extensive where a breakfast of porridge, fish, bacon and egg could be ordered for 3s (15p) and a salmon dinner cost 3s (15p).

P&A Campbell's *Waverley* photographed in the 1930s.

Glen Usk's attractively carved paddle box photographed in May 1939.

Ravenswood arriving at Minehead.

Cardiff Queen (left foreground), *Bristol Queen* (right foreground) and *Glen Usk* (astern) laid up in Penarth Docks in 1961. 1960 had been the final year of service for the *Glen Usk* and she was withdrawn from service by P&A Campbell. With the arrival of the *St Trillo* from North Wales in 1963, *Glen Usk's* future was sealed and she was scrapped in May 1963.

P. & A. CAMPBELL LTD.

SPECIAL ANNOUNCEMENT

MAIDEN VOYAGE of P.S. BRISTOL QUEEN
SATURDAY, September 14th, 1946
BRISTOL to ILFRACOMBE (Direct)

Leave BRISTOL (Hotwells Landing Stage) 9.15 a.m
Leave ILFRACOMBE 5.15 p.m.   Direct to Bristol

CATERING ON BOARD   FARES : Single 11/- Day Return 14/6

Tickets obtainable on Steamer   No Advance Bookings

The Lady Mayoress of Bristol, using a bottle of Bristol Milk Sherry, launched the *Bristol Queen* on Thursday 4 April 1946. Her maiden voyage took place on Saturday 14 September when she departed Bristol at 9.17 a.m. for a cruise to Ilfracombe where she arrived at 1.15 p.m.

Bristol Queen was slightly larger and older than her sister *Cardiff Queen*, and was built by Charles Hill & Sons of Bristol whilst her engines (which were used as a model for *Waverley's*) were built by Rankin & Blackmore of Greenock. She was built to a very high standard, could achieve a speed of 20 knots and could handle with ease the sometimes challenging seas of the Bristol Channel. This photograph shows the Promenade Deck whilst cruising off the Gower Coast.

Captain Jack George at the telegraph and Chief Officer Neville Cottman at the helm of the *Bristol Queen* arriving at Clevedon in September 1953. Earlier that year, *Bristol Queen* was chartered by English Electric at the Coronation Fleet Review at Spithead.

Bristol Queen passing under the Clifton Suspension Bridge at Bristol. *Bristol Queen* offered popular cruises from here along the dramatic North Devon coast to Ilfracombe where a cream tea was an essential part of the day's cruise!

After Sun Lounge aboard the *Bristol Queen*.

Cardiff Queen was the second of a planned four paddle steamers which P&A Campbell intended to build after the Second World War to replace wartime losses. This photograph shows *Cardiff Queen* whilst undertaking her trials on the Firth of Clyde, 12 June 1947. She achieved a speed of just a little over 17 knots. Her trials were undertaken in the same week as *Waverley*'s maiden voyage.

1955 saw the large-scale introduction of entertainment aboard the *Cardiff Queen* and *Bristol Queen* to encourage more passengers to take a cruise. This had been absent since the 1920s and proved to be very popular. Amongst the artistes were a young Shirley Bassey and Acker Bilk.

Cardiff Queen's siren blowing on departure from Padstow in 1966.

Waverley's first visit to the new pier at Lundy in 2001. Before the pier was built, passengers had to be landed by launch, which took a great deal of time as many ferry trips had to be made. Now *Waverley* can disembark a full complement of passengers in minutes.

Opposite: Jeanie Deans approaching Craigendoran 15 April 1963. *Jeanie Deans* was the largest paddle steamer ever built for Craigendoran. Miss Rhoda Forbes Whitelaw, daughter of the LNER Chairman, launched her on 7 April 1931. On her main deck first-class passengers had a spacious light oak lounge with etchings of Scott's 'Heart of Midlothian'. Alongside was a confectionery stall and tearoom. A traditional Clyde dining saloon was positioned below the lounge. Accommodation for second-class passengers was provided forward on the main deck. *Jeanie Deans* had a certificate for 1,714 passengers.

Four
Scotland

The popular *Columba* was built in Clydebank in 1878 and gained her reputation from serving the 'Royal Route' from Glasgow to Ardrishaig for David MacBrayne. During her career she made over 5,600 visits to Ardrishaig. She had the first floating post office, a hairdressers and book and fruit stalls. With her twin cylinder, non-compound oscillating engines, she was rather outdated, but these combined with her large size, still enabled her to continue in service until she was broken up in 1936.

Gondolier on the Caledonian Canal. *Gondolier* was built at Clydebank in 1866. She cruised along the Caledonian Canal between Banavie and Inverness for over seventy years. In 1930 she received the haystack boiler from the redundant *Grenadier*. She carried on for another nine years before being taken over by the Admiralty in 1939, when she was stripped of most of her fittings and equipment before facing a bleak end when she was sunk as a blockship in Scarpa Flow.

The *Fusilier* was built in Paisley by John McArthur & Co. in 1888. *Fusilier* spent most summers at Oban from where she sailed to connect with services on the Caledonian Canal. She also served on the Oban to Crinan route as well as offering short cruises from Oban. From 1927 to 1931 she undertook the Oban to Staffa and Iona cruises. *Fusilier* was sold in the summer of 1934 for sailing's on the Firth of Forth before being sold again in 1935 and renamed *Lady Orme* for cruises from Llandudno to the Menai Straits. In 1936 she undertook cruises out of Ramsgate before returning to North Wales in 1937. The following year she was renamed *Crestawave* before being broken up in 1939.

Duchess of Fife in Rothesay Bay, 1923. The *Duchess of Fife* was very much an Edwardian steamer. She had been built to compete with other steamers in a fiercely competitive era.

Princess May on Loch Lomond. *Princess May* was launched on 11 October 1898. She was one of the first Loch Lomond steamers to have a deck saloon that covered the full width of the hull. The vessel had a fine dining saloon and in the early days each place setting included a paper napkin with a map of Loch Lomond which helped the diners to find where they were, along with a menu and the name of the steward.

Jeanie Deans at Rothesay *c.*1936 with her grey hull livery. *Jeanie Deans* is perhaps one of the most fondly remembered of all Clyde paddle steamers. She was placed on the Upper Clyde, cruising from Craigendoran. In her second season Ayr, Arran and Ailsa Craig were incorporated into her programme. In her latter years she was associated mainly with Arrochar and the Kyles of Bute. She spent her last year of service on the Clyde in 1964 before being withdrawn. She sailed largely and regrettably unsuccessfully, on the Thames as the *Queen of the South* in 1966 and 1967.

A rare photograph of *Waverley* as she enters the waters of the Clyde at her launch in October 1946. *Waverley* was built by A&J Inglis of Glasgow. Lady Matthews, wife of the Chairman of LNER, launched her. *Waverley* cost £160,000 to build and the master for the new vessel was Captain John Cameron DSC, who had commanded the previous *Waverley* which had been sunk at Dunkirk. Charles McLean was Chief Engineer.

By the late 1950s, *Jeanie Deans* was working on her regular 'Round Bute' cruise. On 25 May 1957 she was one of a staggering eight pleasure steamers sailing from Glasgow Bridge Wharf when she joined *Duchess of Hamilton*, *Queen Mary II*, *Caledonia*, *Countess of Breadalbane*, *Duchess of Montrose*, *Maid of Cumbrae* and *Maid of Skelmorlie*.

Holidaymakers arriving after a traditional trip 'Doon the Watter' aboard the *Jupiter* at the ever popular Rothesay in the 1950s. *Jupiter* had been built in Glasgow by Fairfields in 1937 and was designed for the Dunoon and Rothesay services. After war service, she returned to the Clyde in 1946 and later became associated with the Sunday cruises from Glasgow to Lochgoilhead. She remained in service until 1957 and was then withdrawn. It was another four years before she finally went to the inevitable breakers in Dublin in March 1961.

Caledonia undertook her trials on 27 March 1934. Whilst clearly she was a paddle steamer, her paddle boxes were concealed. A favourite of many enthusiasts, *Caledonia* was originally built for service in the Upper Clyde and included afternoon cruises. From 1954 to 1964 she was the Ayr, Troon and Ardrossan steamer. Her last five summers were based at Craigendoran. After being withdrawn in 1969, she was renamed *Old Caledonia* in April 1970 and later became a floating pub and restaurant on the Thames. Tragically she was gutted by fire on 26 April 1980 and was later scrapped at Sittingbourne.

Traditional 'fan boards' aboard the steamers helped to ensure that passengers joined the correct vessel. But as always, there were often a few passengers who managed to get aboard the wrong paddle steamer and found themselves stranded on a pier miles from home. Here the fan boards aboard the *Caledonia* show the destinations for a Millport Illuminations cruise in September 1969.

Caledonia cuts through the waters in this shot photographed from her sponson in September 1961.

Passengers disembarking at Dunoon during a commemorative cruise aboard the *Caledonia* during the 1968 season.

Mate John Ellis docking the *Caledonia* at Tighnabruaich in June 1969.

Right: RMS *Caledonia*, on charter to David MacBrayne, loading mails at Gourock in April 1969. This was the first time for well over thirty years that a paddle steamer had sailed on the Royal Mail route from Gourock to Tarbert.

Below: The *Talisman* at Gourock Pier. *Talisman* was unique as she was driven by direct drive diesel electric machinery. She was launched on 10 April 1935 and during the Second World War became HMS *Aristocrat*. After a refit, she re-entered service in 1946 on her Craigendoran-based Upper Clyde sailing's. She made her last public sailing (to Kilmun) on 17 November 1966 and was broken up at Dalmuir in 1967.

Above: Talisman on 15 May 1965 at Wemyss Bay, celebrating the centenary of the Wemyss Bay railway.

Left: Maid of the Loch disembarking passengers at Balloch Pier on Loch Lomond. Like *Waverley, Maid of the Loch* was built by A &J Inglis at Glasgow and was transported in sections by rail from Glasgow to Balloch to be re-assembled at the lochside. *Maid of the Loch* was the last paddle steamer to be built in the UK. The ship is now being restored for eventual operation on Loch Lomond once again.

LOCH LOMOND
STEAMER SERVICES
EXCURSIONS and TOURS

P.S. "MAID OF THE LOCH"

26th MAY until
14th SEPTEMBER, 1958
(except Wednesday 28th and Friday 30th May)

THE CALEDONIAN STEAM PACKET COMPANY LIMITED
in association with
BRITISH RAILWAYS

Brochure for Loch Lomond steamer services offered by the *Maid of the Loch* during the 1958 season. Day tours were offered including the famous Three Lochs tour as well as evening circular tours from Glasgow, whereby passengers departed from Glasgow by train at 3.00 p.m. to Ardlui. *Maid of the Loch* then took them on a one hour twenty minute cruise to Balloch where they joined a train back to Glasgow to arrive at 9.50 p.m.

Maid of the Loch cruising the waters of Loch Lomond.

Left: HM Queen Elizabeth II disembarks from the *Maid of the Loch* after a cruise in 1971. Both the Queen and the Duke of Edinburgh had cruised before on the *Maid of the Loch* in 1965.

Below: Jeanie Deans at Arrochar during her last ever call in 1964. The end of an era came on the 28 September 1964 when *Jeanie Deans* returned from Rothesay to Wemyss Bay with a compliment of trippers during the Glasgow September holiday. In the following March, she was offered for sale to face an uncertain future.

Right: The promenade deck of *Waverley* c.1970. *Waverley* had spent the first part of her career in relative obscurity. The *Jeanie Deans* and other Clyde paddle steamers more often stole the limelight. But by the early 1970s, things were changing. Many people started to realize the 'uniqueness' of *Waverley*. 'Heritage' was starting to become a marketable product. All of this led to her preservation in 1974. It is doubtful whether those involved in those early uncertain days ever saw a life for *Waverley* into the twenty-first century, or could have imagined the £4 million invested in her heritage rebuild in 2000.

Below: Waverley approaching Rothesay in 1971. Rothesay is still a popular destination on a trip 'Doon the Watter'.

Left: Entertainment has always been a strong feature of a paddle steamer cruise. Here Charlie Harkin's band entertains passengers aboard *Waverley* in the 1970s.

Below: Waverley's Dining Saloon *c.*1970. At this time, the saloon had changed very little since *Waverley's* maiden voyage in 1947. Passengers still booked their places for meals which were cooked on a coal-fired range and served in the Clyde tradition, but by the late 1970s, the character was destroyed by bland modernization. Thankfully, with some modifications, the interior of the dining saloon was restored to its 1947 glory in 2000, although it is now self-service.

Right: Waverley's paddle box photographed whilst she was alongside at Arrochar in June 1970. During this period her paddle box was painted white but in 1972 her owners, the Caledonian Steam Packet Co., agreed that her unique status as the last sea-going paddle steamer should be accentuated by painting her paddle boxes black, almost as they were in her earliest days.

Below: Waverley at Lochranza on 4 September 1971.

Left: During the 1972 season *Waverley* offered cruises to Arrochar, Tarbert, Round Bute as well as 'Round the Lochs' and Firth of Clyde. It was possible to obtain lunch for 75p and high tea for 60p. The 'uniqueness' of *Waverley* was at last being appreciated at this time as shown by this brochure.

Below: Waverley departing from Rothesay. In 1973, *Waverley's* normal service included the cruise Round Bute on Sundays, Mondays and Thursdays from Gourock, as her home at Craigendoran had closed after the 1972 season. On Fridays, she cruised to Tarbert and on Tuesdays and Wednesdays she did the Round the Lochs cruise. Saturdays were spent on ferry service with an afternoon cruise to Tighnabruaich.

Above: Waverley at Tobermory. Waverley made her first visit to the Hebridean Islands of Scotland in 1981. She made her first call at Tobermory, 'capital' of the Isle of Mull in 1983.

Right: Waverley's steam whistle in Caledonian MacBrayne days just prior to her preservation in 1974.

Roddy McIsaac was *Waverley's* Bosun from 1976 until his early retirement twenty years later. Roddy was one of *Waverley's* characters and was well known around the whole of the UK for his friendliness and sense of humour. He was also the man who steered *Waverley* as she approached piers around the UK's coastline.

Commerative Cruise
celebrating the launch of the

PADDLE STEAMER

WAVERLEY

Friday 18th October 1996
Grand Evening Buffet Cruise
with Jazz Band

Departure: 7 p.m.
Arrive back 10.30 p.m.

TICKET: £29

21

The Launch of the Paddle Steamer WAVERLEY at Inglis Yard, 2nd October 1946

Souvenir ticket for the special cruise to commemorate the fiftieth anniversary of *Waverley's* launch held on 18 October 1996.

Waverley made her first visit to Fort William in 1982. She was the first paddle steamer since 1939 to cruise amongst the majestic scenery of Loch Linnhe and to pass the stunning scenery of Appin and Ben Cruachan to Oban.

Waverley at anchor in the Sound of Iona as her passengers are ferried ashore to the Sacred Isle where St Columba landed in AD 563, bringing Christianity to Britain from Ireland.

Waverley resplendent in August 2000 after the first phase of her Heritage Rebuild. The steamer is seen here at Rothesay just a couple of days after her return to the Clyde. *Waverley* was enormously popular at that time as thousands flocked to see the quality of the restoration work.

Five
Elsewhere

The *Bickerstaffe* shown against Blackpool Tower *c*.1900. One of the finest paddle steamers of her day, she was in service for nearly fifty years. John Bickerstaffe had formed the Blackpool Passenger Steamboat Co. in December 1894 to help finance the construction of the *Queen of the North* which entered service in 1895. The *Bickerstaffe* lasted until being broken up in 1928 whilst the *Queen of the North* was lost during the First World War. With the withdrawal of the *Bickerstaffe*, pleasure steamer cruises on the Lancashire coast declined and despite efforts to re-introduce new vessels, the service ended in the late 1940s.

Pleasure steamer cruises were a popular feature of Blackpool's holiday trade from the mid-1860s until the Second World War. Such favourites as *Greyhound*, *Queen of the North*, *Bickerstaffe* and *Queen of the Bay* offered services from the rival North and Central piers to such destinations as the Isle of Man, Llandudno, Southport and Liverpool. The Bickerstaffe family who built the famous Blackpool Tower in 1894, operated a lot of the steamers.

Taking photographs of passengers aboard the paddle steamers cruising across Morecambe Bay from Fleetwood to Barrow-in-Furness was quite common. Here passengers are seen aboard the *Lady Moyra* for a day in the Lake District just before the First World War.

Grand Day Sea Excursions.

AN IDEAL MARINE EXCURSION
Through the Picturesque MENAI STRAITS.

SUPERB VIEW of the FAMOUS
Suspension and Tubular Bridges.

BEAUMARIS, BANGOR
AND MENAI BRIDGE TO

CARNARVON

(With ample time Ashore to visit its Historic and Famous Castle.)

Each Week Day,
August 25th to 30th.

By the Favourite Saloon Steamer "SNOWDON" (Weather and circumstances permitting)

("ST. TRILLO," Tuesday and Saturday).

		† Monday, St. Trillo	Tues. to Saturday, Snowdon or St. Trillo						Each Week Day.
BEAUMARIS	dep.	11 45 a.m.	12 0 noon	CARNARVON	...	...	dep.	*3 0 p.m.
BANGOR	...	12 0 noon	12 20 p.m.	MENAI BRIDGE	...	...	...	*3 45 "
		Snowdon						
MENAI BRIDGE	...	12 30 p.m.	12 30 "	BANGOR	...	...	...	*4 0 "
CARNARVON	arr.	1 15 "	1 15 "	BEAUMARIS	...	...	arr.	*4 15 "

*Note.—Time leaving may vary. Correct time to be obtained on board the Steamer.

† On Monday, Beaumaris and Bangor passengers leave by "St. Trillo," transferring at Menai Bridge to "Snowdon" for Carnarvon.

BOAT AND RAIL.—Passengers with Steamer Tickets desirous of a longer stay ashore can also return from Carnarvon by any train upon surrendering the return half of their Steamboat ticket to the booking clerk and paying 4d, in exchange for which a 3rd class single ticket will be issued to Menai Bridge or Bangor.

DAY FARES (INCLUDING PIER DUES)—	1st SALOON. Single.	1st SALOON. Return.	2nd SALOON. Single	2nd SALOON. Return
Beaumaris to Carnarvon	2/-	2/6	1/6	2/-
Bangor to Carnarvon	1/9	2/3	1/3	1/9
Menai Bridge to Carnarvon	1/6	2/-	1/-	1/6
Beaumaris to Bangor or Menai Bridge...	9d	1/-		

(Children over 3 and under 12 years half fare.)   EXCELLENT CATERING ON BOARD.

All Tickets are issued and Goods carried subject to the Company's Conditions of Carriage, as exhibited at the Company's Office and on the Steamers.

For all further information apply to the Company's Agent, W. STANLEY, Beaumaris (Tel. No. 4 Beaumaris); also Pier Gates, Bangor (Tel. 12) and Menai Bridge (Tel. 29); T. S. INGHAM, Market Street and High Street, Carnarvon; or to the Liverpool and North Wales S.S. Co. Ltd., T. G. BREW, Secretary, 40 Chapel Street, Liverpool.

For particulars of other Sailings, see Bills at Pier Gates.

RAIL and SEA TRIPS to CARNARVON and back.

Day Excursion Tickets will be issued until further notice, from
BEAUMARIS, BANGOR and MENAI BRIDGE
(Weather and circumstances permitting.)

Outward—		Monday, St. Trillo	Tuesday to Saturday Snowdon or St. Trillo	Homeward—Passengers may return from Carnarvon by any Ordinary Train.
Beaumaris	...dep.	11 45 a.m.	12 0 noon	
Bangor ...	...	12 0 noon	12 20 p.m.	Beaumaris passengers must find their own means of conveyance from Menai Bridge or Bangor Railway Stations.
		Snowdon		
Menai Bridge		12 30 p.m.	12 30 "	
Carnarvon	...arr.	1 15 "	1 15 "	

Return Fares 2/1 Beaumaris or Bangor and Carnarvon } Saloon on Steamer
   "   "   1/7 Menai Bridge and Carnarvon - - } 6d extra.

Tickets available day of issue only. No Luggage allowed.

Excursion Tickets are only available to and from the Stations named upon them, and any Passenger using them on the Outward or Return Journey at any Station short of, or beyond the Stations named upon them, or travelling by any other train than those mentioned on the Excursion bills, will forfeit the Ticket and be charged the Ordinary Fare.

The contract and liability of each Company or Proprietor are limited to their own Railway, Coaches, or Steamboats, and their Tickets are issued subject to the conditions and regulations referred to in the Time Tables, Books, Bills and Notices of the respective Companies and Proprietors on whose Railways, Coaches, or Steamboats such Tickets are available.

(451)   ☞ BOOK AT PIER GATES. ☜

Snowdon was built by Laird Brothers of Birkenhead in 1892 for the Snowdon Passenger Steamboat Co. for service along the North Wales coast. She had a passenger certificate for 462 and a speed of 14 knots. She was a fine looking paddle steamer with the bridge forward of the funnel and an awning that could be rolled out to protect passengers from bad weather. She was acquired by the Liverpool & North Wales Co. in 1899. During the First World War she served as a minesweeper from Harwich and Dover and resumed North Wales cruises in 1920. In September 1930 she undertook a series of cruises from Blackpool. She was broken up in 1931 at Port Glasgow.

Previous Page: Handbill for cruises offered by *Snowdon* and *St Trillo* in the early years of the twentieth century. Cruises were offered to Carnarvon from Beaumaris, Bangor and Menai Bridge. On some cruises, the outward journey was by *St Trillo* and the return by *Snowdon*. On other cruises the return leg of the journey was by train.

Departure of " La Marguerite," Menai Bridge

La Marguerite spent the first part of her career on the Thames. A large vessel, she was over twice the tonnage of any other paddle steamer on the North Wales service. She had a passenger capacity of 2,077 and had been built in Glasgow by Fairfields in 1894. The Liverpool & North Wales Co. placed her on the Menai Straits run from Liverpool. *La Marguerite* was the second largest paddle steamer ever to operate in British waters (IOMSPC's *Empress Queen* being the largest).

La Marguerite departing from Beaumaris. After service during the First World War she resumed her North Wales cruises in 1920. Although she was a prestigious ship, she must have been uneconomic for the North Wales Co. and she was replaced by the turbine driven *St Tudno* in 1926. *La Marguerite* was scrapped at Briton Ferry after just twenty-one years' service.

Llandudno was a popular destination for cruises along the North Wales coast. The pier was built in 1876 and is regarded as one of the UK's finest Victorian piers. Calls are still made by the *Waverley* and *Balmoral*.

St Elvies was built for the Liverpool & North Wales Co. in 1896. She could carry 991 passengers and had a speed of just over 18 knots. *St Elvies* undertook cruises from Liverpool and Llandudno round Anglesey and between Llandudno and the Isle of Man. She also offered excursions from Liverpool to Llandudno. After service as a minesweeper during the First World War, *St Elvies* returned to North Wales service in March 1919 and then spent another eleven years in service there before being broken up at Birkenhead at the end of the 1930 season.

St Tudno was launched in April 1891 and was a very popular paddle steamer on the North Wales service. She could carry 1,061 passengers and had a speed of 19 knots. She ran cruises from Liverpool to the Welsh coast as well as a few trips from Llandudno to the Isle of Man.

King George operated on the River Conway and entered service in 1891. She was the last paddle steamer in service at Conway. She was laid up in 1940 and was scrapped soon afterwards. The Conway steamers all had yellow funnels with a black top.

Lincoln Castle was built by Inglis of Glasgow and entered service in 1940. She was built as a passenger and vehicle ferry for the Hull to New Holland crossing on the River Humber. With her sisters *Tattershall Casle* and *Wingfield Castle* she also undertook cruises in the area. She was due to continue operation until the opening of the Humber Bridge but boiler problems caused her early withdrawal. *Lincoln Castle* is now statically preserved.

Above: Wingfield Castle was launched on 24 September 1934. She could carry sixteen cars and 1,200 passengers. As well as being a ferry, *Wingfield Castle* also carried out numerous excursions from Hull to Grimsby as well as from Spurn Head and offered evening cruises until finishing in 1968. *Wingfield Castle* was sold in 1974.

Right: Handbill for a Paddle Steamer Preservation Society cruise aboard the *Lincoln Castle* in August 1975.

Paddle Steamer Preservation Society

Come Aboard!
for a special public
STEAMBOAT CRUISE
on the
Rivers Humber and Trent
by the Sealink Steamer
P. S. 'Lincoln Castle'
on
Sunday 3rd August, 1975

TIMES

Dep. 13.50   NEW HOLLAND   arr. 18.15
Dep. 14.20   HULL (Corporation Pier)   arr. 18.40

Thence cruise up the River Humber, passing Hull Docks, the new Humber Bridge and proceeding up the River Trent towards Flixborough. The cruise is non-landing.

FARES

Adults £1.70   Children (under 14) £1.00

(Adults £1.50, Children 90p, if booked prior to sailing day)

Special rates for parties of 10 or more
ADVANCE BOOKING IS ADVISED
TEAS AND REFRESHMENTS AVAILABLE ON BOARD. LICENSED BAR OPEN DURING THE CRUISE. AMPLE COVERED ACCOMMODATION FOR ALL PASSENGERS
OPPORTUNITY TO WATCH THE FASCINATING COAL-FIRED STEAM RECIPROCATING ENGINES

Cruise arranged with the co-operation of Sealink.

Passengers are carried subject to the advertised conditions of carriage applicable to vessels of the British Railways Board, operated on the Hull/New Holland Ferry. The sailing is subject to weather and circumstance permitting.

FURTHER INFORMATION OVERLEAF

What better way to end this book looking at the photographic heritage of paddle steamers than to look to the future. *Waverley* is seen departing from her Heritage Rebuild for her sea trials at Great Yarmouth in August 2000. The *Jeanie Deans, Consul, Golden Eagle* and *Cardiff Queen* may be no more, but at least with the *Waverley* and *Kingswear Castle* we are still able to savour the type of day beloved by our forefathers. It is good to reflect that the photographic heritage will continue!